BREATH

harmony of prana

Debiprasad
MA Yoga

suryastra

ISBN: 978-81-903678-6-8

Breath

Copyright © Debiprasad

First Edition : 2008   Price : Rs. 45

Published by
Suryastra
C-43, First Floor
Green Park Main
New Delhi - 110016
India

www.suryastra.com

Email: info@suryastra.com

Printed by Shivam Sundram
E-9 Green Park Extn
New Delhi -110016
India

EDITOR'S NOTE

Breath is the bridge between the cosmos and our being.

This occurs through respiration the breathing process consisting of inspiration and expiration.

Inhalation and exhalation of breath occurs throughout the breathing passage, the nose and mouth, through the throat and into the lungs. Here the breath meets with blood to exchange its contents.

Our being as we know it ceases to exist without breath, yet what is contained within breath continues.

Einstein claimed that energy and mass are relative which means that they are one and the same thing.

Energy is neither created nor destroyed it merely changes from one form into another.

1st Law of Physics

Science itself is rooted in the discussion of energy. Cultures with their languages have evolved over time giving different terms to name this life force. The Chinese term may be 'chi' and the Indian term 'prana.'

This book is an attempt to discuss the term prana, its flow and ways we can create harmony and wellbeing.

Acknowledgements

Dr. Anuj Agarwal
    MBBS *(London)*

CONTENTS

PRANA	7
ASANA	9
PREPARATORY PRACTISE OF PRANAYAMA	39
PRANAYAMA	43
THE FLOW OF PRANA	54
HARMONY	57

PRANA

Prana is the subtle force working through life, creation and the being.

No action is possible without the force of prana.

In essence the energy is neither created nor destroyed, it merely changes from one form into another.

Consciousness cannot manifest without prana. Prana cannot exist without consciousness.

It is the energy that is working throughout the being.

Prana flows through subtle channels and it ensures the health and wellbeing of the body. Disease results when the flow of prana is blocked in its channels subsequently accumulating toxins. The variety of systems important to life, such as breathing, circulation, digestion, movement, reproduction and mental processes are controlled by the flow of prana.

Feelings, sensitivity, emotions, will power and thought are all directed by the prana. Imbalance in the flow of prana due to emotional problems and lifestyle causes nervous tension resulting in fear and depression of the being.

Prana flowing through its channels also flows throughout the body and it is possible to control this through one's breath.
Breath enters and leaves our body primarily through the nostrils of our nose.

When the flow of breath is balanced through both nostrils then there will be a harmony in the being. This can be created through an understanding of pranayama.

Pranayama may be understood as the state of being where the flow of prana is in harmony.

Mental thoughts affect the prana which in turn changes the breath. When calm the breath is rhythmic, and when one has tension the breath becomes restless.

Just as thoughts affect the breath, so breath affects the thoughts.

By understanding pranayama the breath can be used through awareness to direct the flow of prana and so affecting the thoughts.

Pranayama includes the awareness of breathing to direct the prana.

This awareness is linked with the subtle aspects of the being, consisting of consciousness, mind and the cells of the body.

Emotional problems and an imbalanced lifestyle blocks the flow of prana.

Prevention of this is possible through physical movements, breath and awareness which are collectively known as asana.

Asana aims to allow the proper flow of prana throughout the body. When prana flows in harmony, toxins are removed from the system ensuring health and wellbeing.

ASANA

Asana is any such form that allows one to feel steady and comfortable.
Unless the body and breath becomes comfortable and steady it is difficult to bring the being in harmony.

Everyone's body condition is different so one needs to be aware and understand the nature of their being.

Here are some common forms of asana one can use.

savasana

Lie down with the back on the floor.
Keep the body straight from head to toe
Legs slightly apart and the arms a little away from the body
The palms of the hands turned upwards
Adjust the body position and clothes, until comfortable
Close the eyes.
Watch the breath
Become aware of the body
Consciously relax each and every part
From toe to head

sitting on a chair

Sit on a chair with hands on knees or an arm rest.
Legs shoulder width apart.
Feet flat on the ground or on a foot rest.
Head, neck and spine should be straight.
Close the eyes and relax the whole body.

sukhasana

Sit on the floor with the legs straight.
Bend the right leg and place the foot under the left thigh.
Bend the left leg and place the foot under the right thigh.
Place the hands on the knees.
Keep the back and neck straight.
Close the eyes and relax the whole body.

vajrasana

Stand on the knees.
Keep the toes flat
Sit between the heels
Place the hands on the knees.
Keep the back and neck straight.
Close the eyes.

Remain for a few minutes and watch the breath
Be aware of the organs of digestion

ardha padmasana

Sit on the floor with the legs straight.
Bend one leg and place the foot on top of the opposite thigh.
Bend the other leg and place the sole of the foot on the inside of the opposite thigh.

padmasana

Sit on the floor with the legs straight.
Bend one leg and place the foot on top of the opposite thigh.
Then bend the other leg and place the foot on top of the opposite thigh.
Both the heels should be close to the pubic bone and both knees should touch the ground in the final position.
The head and spine should be straight.
Place the hands on the knees.
Close the eyes and relax the whole body

Here are some breathing movements to bring about a harmony between the body movements and breath. They will help to increase the passage of breath available.

hands in and out

Stand with the feet together
Keep the hands in front of the body
Palms together
Inhale while stretch the arms out to the side as far as is possible
Exhale while returning the arms in front
Repeat 5 times

hands stretching

Stand with the feet together
Interlock the fingers
Place the palms on the chest
Inhale while stretching the arms with the palms facing outwards
Exhale while returning the arms, bringing the hands to the chest
Repeat 5 times

ankle stretching

Stand with feet together
Place the palms in front of the thighs
Inhale while raising the arms over the head
Simultaneously raise the heels from the ground
Standing on the toes
Exhale while lowering the heels and arms
Repeat 5 times

backward and forward bending

Stand with legs shoulder width apart
Place the palms in front of the thighs
Inhale while raising the arms over the heed and bend backwards
Exhale while bending forwards with the arms
Try to touch the floor
Repeat 5 times

After prolonged lack of movement, the flow of prana gets blocked in certain joints resulting in stiffness, muscular tension, lack of proper blood flow and minor functional defects.

pawanmuktasana

This helps to loosen the joints removing any blockage and allowing the free flow of prana in the being. It can be practiced at any time of the day.
Repeat each of the movements for each joint five times.
The movements should be slow and smooth with breath and awareness.

Sit on the floor in a comfortable asana.
Close the eyes and become aware of the body.
Find out exactly how the body is feeling, whether it is experiencing any pain, discomfort or any other sensation.
Gently open the eyes.
Stretch the legs in front of the body.
Place the palms on the floor.
The back, neck and head should be straight.

toe bending

Be aware of the toes.
Move the toes slowly backward and forward.
Inhale as the toes move backward
Exhale as the toes move forward
Be aware on the stretching sensation.

ankle bending

Slowly move both feet backward and forward
Bend from the ankle joints
Inhale as the feet move backward
Exhale as the feet move forward
Be aware on the ankle joints and calf muscles

ankle rotation

Keep the feet separated
Slowly rotate both feet from the ankles together
But in opposite directions.
Repeat in the opposite direction.
Inhale on the upward movement
Exhale on the downward movement
Be aware on the rotation of the ankle joint

knee rending

Keep the hands under the thighs.
Do not allow the heel or toes to touch the floor.
Bend the left knee so that the heel comes close to the buttocks.
Then slowly straighten.
Practice with the left leg

Repeat with the right leg.
Inhale while bending the leg.
Exhale while straightening the leg.
Be aware on the knee joint and thigh muscles

knee rotation

Bend the left knee as in knee bending above.
Keep the hands under the left thigh while interlocking the fingers.
Rotate the lower leg from the knee in a large circular movement.
The upper leg and trunk should be still.
Rotate clockwise
And then anti-clockwise.
Repeat with right leg.
Inhale on the upward movement
Exhale on the downward movement
Be aware of the knee joint.

fingers clenching

Keep the hands in front.
Clench the fingers into a fist
Then release the fingers from the fist
Inhale while clenching the fingers.
Exhale while releasing the fingers.
Be aware of the finger joints.

wrist rotation

Make a fist and rotate clockwise
Then rotate anti–clockwise.
Inhale on upward movement.
Exhale on downward movement.
Be aware of the wrist joint.

elbows bending

Keep the arms in front
Palm facing upwards.
Bend at the elbows and touch the shoulders.
Then straighten the arms back in front.
Inhale while bending the arm.
Exhale while straightening the arm.
Be aware of the elbow joint.

shoulder rotation

Keep the fingers on the shoulders
Rotate from back to front
Repeat from front to back.
Inhale on upward movement
Exhale on downward movement.
Be aware of the shoulder joint.

neck movements

Bend backward
Bend forward
Inhale while bending backward
Exhale while bending forward

Keep neck straight in the centre.
Bend to the left.
Return to centre
Bend to the right.
Return to the centre.
Inhale while bending to the side
Exhale while returning to the centre.

Rotate the neck clockwise.
Repeat anti-clockwise.
Inhale on backward movement
Exhale on forward movement

Be aware of the neck joint.

While practicing asana and pranayama one should remember the following:

- *Practise under guidance of a yoga practitioner*
- *Morning is preferable as the stomach and bowels are empty. One can practice anytime though there should be a gap of at least three hours after eating.*
- *Choose a well ventilated space with passing air*
- *Wear loose clothing*
- *Consult a physician or yoga consultant if there are any health problems*
- *Avoid straining*
- *Gradually increase the length of time in each posture, according to your own physical capacity.*
- *While holding a posture allow the breath to be continuous*
- *During each asana remain aware of the part of the body where there is a stretch or pain.*
- *After completing each asana feel the after effect in the being.*

SUPINE POSTURES

base position

Lie flat on the back with the legs together and straight.
The arms should be by the sides, palm down and head, neck and spine in a straight line.

pristhabhumitadasana

Lie in the base position
Slowly stretch both arms above the head with palms facing upward.
Now stretch the upper part of the body with the hands and the lower part of the body with the toes.
Remain for a few seconds then come back to savasana.
Inhale while stretching the hands.
Exhale while returning back.
Be aware on the stretching muscles.

suptapawanmuktasana

Lie in the base position
Bend the right knee and bring it to the abdomen.
Interlock the fingers and clasp the hands on and below the right knee.
Press the right knee to the abdomen.
The left leg should be straight and on the ground.
Now slowly raise the head and shoulders from the ground and try to touch the nose with the right knee.
Remain for a few seconds.
Don't hold the breath
Then slowly bringing the head down, straighten the right leg and come to savasana.
Take 2 -3 normal breaths then repeat with the left leg.
Then repeat with both legs.
Exhale while pressing the knees to chest.
Inhale while bringing back the head to the floor.
Be aware of the pressure on the abdomen.

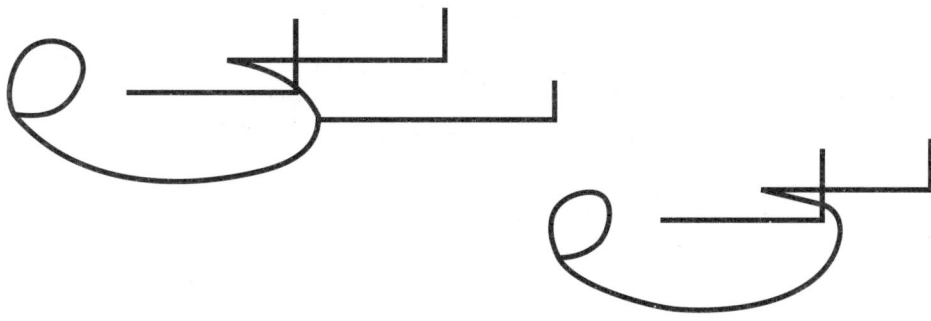

sethubandhasana

Lie in the base position
Slowly bend the knees, bringing your feet towards your buttocks
Slowly lift the hips from the ground
Pull up the hips as much as possible
Push out the abdomen
In this position the chest will touch the chin
Remain for a few seconds
Slowly lower the hips
Return to savasana
Inhale while lifting the hips
Exhale while lowering the hips
Be aware of the abdomen region, back and throat

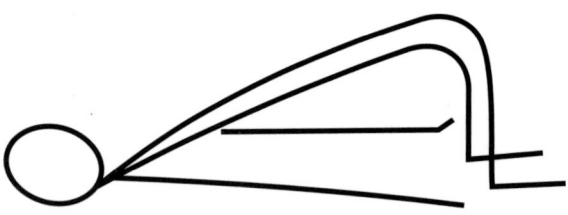

meruvakrasana

Lie in the base position.
Stretch arms sideways parallel to the shoulders.
Palms on the ground
Place the left foot on the right knee
Bring the left knee down to the right side
Try touching the right knee to the floor by twisting from the waist
Twist the neck in the opposite direction
Look at the left hand
Remain for a few seconds
Return to the base position
Change leg
Repeat in the opposite direction
Return to savasana
Inhale while twisting the body
Exhale while returning.
Be aware on the twisting of the abdominal muscles and organs.

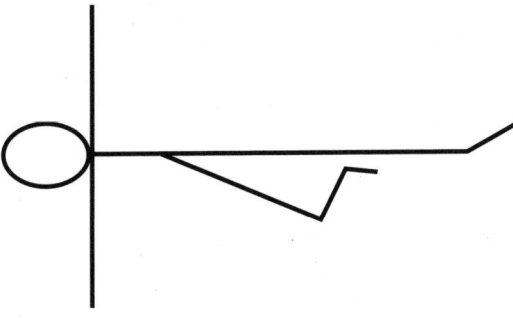

naukasana

Lie in the base position
Bring the arms over the head and stretch
Stretch the toes
Slowly raise the arms, head and shoulders
Keeping the spine straight
Slightly raise the legs about 15cm from the ground
Remain for a few seconds
Return to savasana
Inhale while raising the body
Exhaling while returning
Be aware of the tension in the abdominal region

PRONE POSTURES

base position

Lie down on the abdomen.
Keep the arms along the body
Feet together
Chin on the floor

makarasana

Base position
Bring the arms in front of the forehead.
Place the palms one on top of the other
Keep the forehead on the hands
Legs slightly apart
Relax the whole body
Inhale deeply
Exhale deeply
Be aware of the abdominal movement

bhujangasana

Base position
Place the palms flat on the floor, by the side of the shoulders
Slowly raise the head, neck and chest without taking support of the hands.
Now create a little pressure with the hands doing a maximum stretch backwards
Remain for a few seconds
Return to makarasana
Inhale while rising.
Exhale while coming down
Be aware of the back and breathing through the lungs.

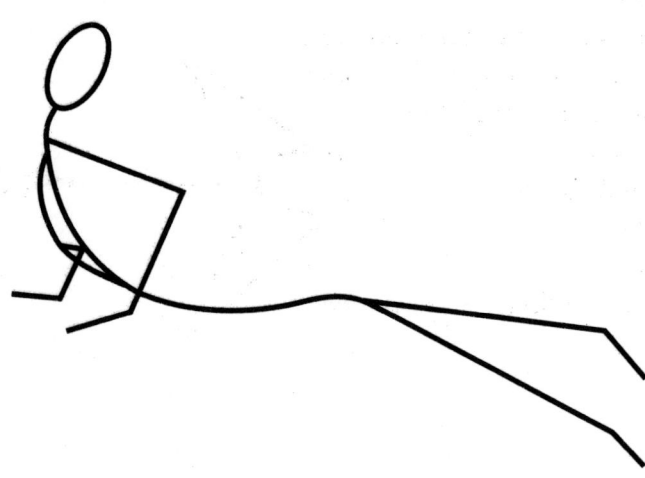

salabhasana

Base position
Place the hands under the thighs
Slowly raise the left leg as much as possible
Keep the left knee straight
Stretch the left toe
Remain for a few seconds
Slowly lower the leg
Repeat with the right leg
Then repeat with both legs
Return to makarasana
Inhale while rising
Exhale while coming down
Be aware of the lower back, abdomen and central chest.

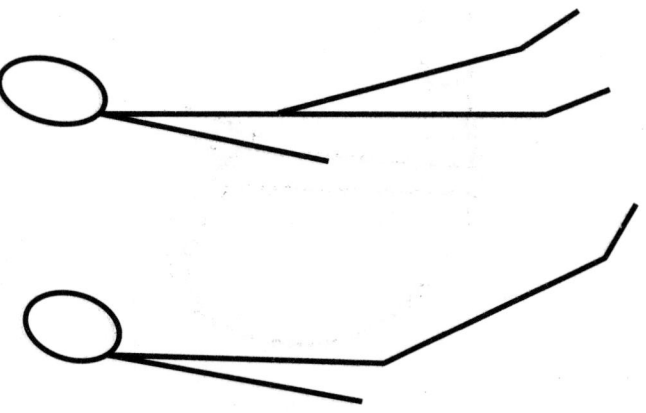

dhanurasana

Base position
Bend the knees bringing the heels to the buttocks
Hold the ankles with the hands
Raise the head, neck, chest and thighs from the ground
In this position the arms will be straight
Try to pull up the body as much as possible
Only the abdomen will remain on the floor
Remain for a few seconds
Return to makarasana
Inhale while pulling the body
Exhale while releasing the body
Be aware of the back, arms and abdomen.

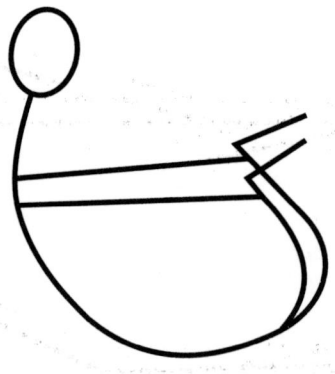

SITTING POSTURES

paschimottanasana

Sit on the floor with legs stretched out straight in front
Place the hands on the knees
Keep the back and neck straight
Slowly raise the arms over the head
Keep the elbows straight, stretching the fingers
Slowly bend forward
Try to hold the toes or ankles without bending the knees
Bring the forehead towards the knees as far as is possible
Remain for a few seconds
Slowly return and bring the arms above the head.
Return to the start position
Inhale while raising the arms above the head
Exhale while bending forward
Be aware of the strain in the knees and lower abdomen

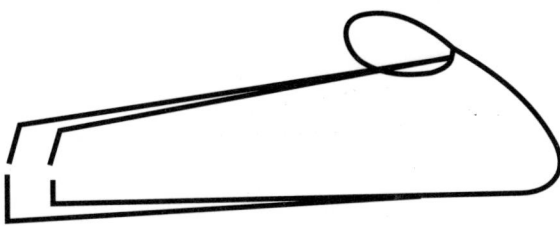

ustrasana

Stand on the knees
Keep a little distance between them
Keep the toes flat
Bend backwards bringing the hands on the heels
Bend the neck backwards
Remain for a few seconds
Slowly return to start position
Inhale while bending backwards
Exhale while returning
Be aware of the spine and upper chest

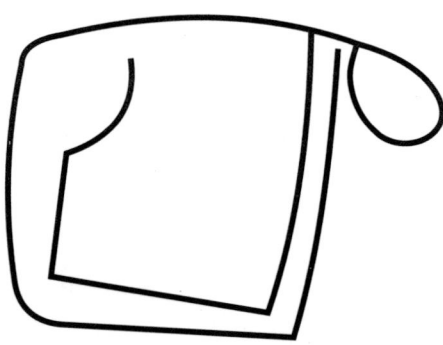

shasankasana

Sit in vajrasana
Place the hands on the knees
Keep the back and neck straight
Slowly raise the arms over the head
Slowly bend forward
Place the palms and forehead on the floor
Keep the elbows slightly bent
Remain for a few seconds
Return to vajrasana.
Inhale while raising the arms
Exhale while bending forwards
Be aware of the blood flow in the head

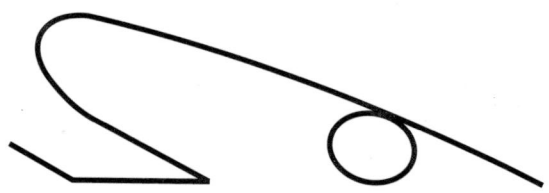

marjariasana

Stand on the knees.
Bend forward.
Keep the hands on the floor in line with the shoulders
Keep the elbows straight
Bring the spine upwards
Bend the neck forwards
Touch the chin to the chest
Remain for a few seconds
Bring the spine downwards
Raising the head and neck
Remain for a few seconds
Return to start position
Exhale while bringing spine up
Inhale while bringing spine down
Be aware of the movement of the spine

STANDING POSTURES

Base position

Stand with feet together
Arms along the body
Keep the neck and back straight

tadasana

Stand in the base position
Interlock the fingers
Turn the hands with the palms facing downwards
Slowly raise the arms over the head.
Simultaneously raise the heels from the ground.
Balance on the toes.
Remain for a few seconds
Return to the base position and relax
Inhale while raising the arms
Exhale while lowering the arms
Be aware of the stretching muscles in the whole body.

triyaktadasana

Stand in base position
Keep the legs shoulder width apart.
Interlock the fingers
Turn the hands with the palms facing downwards
Slowly raise the arms over the head
Bend to the right side.
Remain for a few seconds.
Return to the centre
Repeat to the left side
Bring the arms down and relax
Inhale while bending to the side
Exhale while returning to the centre
Be aware of the side muscles of the body

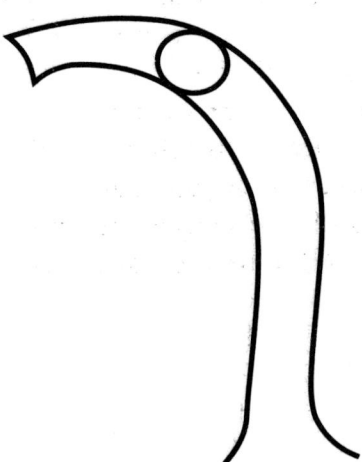

katichakrasana

Stand in base position
Keep the legs a little more than shoulder width apart
Stretch the arms parallel to the shoulders
Slowly twist to the left side from the waist
Legs should remain fixed
Look at the left hand fingers
Remain for a few seconds
Return twisting to the centre
Repeat twisting to the right side
Returning to the centre
Bring the arms down and relax
Inhale while twisting to the side
Exhale while returning to the centre
Be aware of the waist area

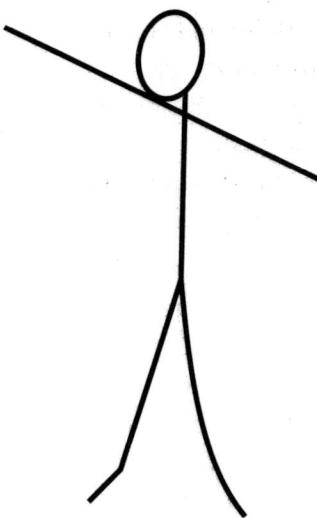

vrikshasana

Stand in base position
Bend the right knee
Hold the right ankle with the right hand
Place the right sole to the left thigh
The heel should be close to the pubic bone
Slowly bring the arms over the head
Keep the palms together
Look at one point
Try to maintain balance holding the body still
Remain for a few seconds or longer
Slowly bring the hands down
Keep the right ankle down
Repeat with other leg
Return to base position and relax
Breathe normally
Be aware of maintaining balance

INVERTED POSTURES

sarvangasana

Lie in the supine posture
Slowly raise the legs over the head
Raise the hips and back
Place the palms on the lower back
Try to straighten the body from shoulders to toes
Point the toes upwards
Remain for a few seconds
Slowly bend the knees
Gently lower the back, then hips
Return to savasana
Breathe normally
Be aware of the blood flow to the head

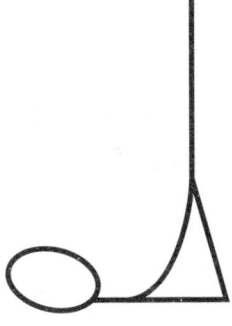

matsyasana

Lie in the supine posture
Stretch the toes
Place the palms flat on the floor by the ears
Fingers towards the body
Lift the chest slightly taking the head back
Bring the crown of the head to the floor
Now bring the hands to the thighs
Remain for a few seconds
Then brings the palms back by the ears
Gently bring the head back to the supine posture.
Return to savasana
Breathe deeply
Be aware of the chest, neck and top of the head

PREPARATORY PRACTISE OF PRANAYAMA

Before starting pranayama we need to prepare the lungs and diaphragm. This will involve the abdomen and chest.

When breathing normally we never use our lungs and diaphragm completely. Through this practice we aim to use the whole passage of breath.

Here are some of the abdominal and chest breathing processes that we are going to practice with a mental count to give an idea on length of time and quantity of breath.

abdominal breathing

Lie down in savasana
Close the eyes.
Become aware of the body.
Be aware on the natural breath that is flowing through the nostrils.
The breath should be effortless
When breathing in, know the breath is flowing in
When breathing out, know the breath is flowing out
Now place the right hand on the abdomen just above the navel and the left hand over the centre of the chest
Inhale while expanding the abdomen as much as possible without expanding the rib cage

Mentally counting 1 to 5
Exhale while contracting the abdominal muscles
Mentally counting 1 to 5
Be aware of the abdominal movements
Repeat 5 to 10 rounds

chest breathing

Inhale while expanding the chest without expanding the abdomen
Mentally counting 1 to 5
Exhale while contracting the chest
Mentally counting 1 to 5
Be aware of the chest movements
Repeat 5 to 10 rounds

abdominal and chest breathing

Inhale while expanding the abdomen
Counting 1 to 5
Then expanding the chest
Counting 6 to 10
Exhale by relaxing the chest
Counting 1 to 5
Relaxing the abdomen
Counting 6 to 10
Repeat 5 to 10 rounds

Retention of breath is for the advanced, and to be carried out under guidance of the yoga practitioner.

abdominal and chest breathing with retention

Inhale while expanding the abdomen
Counting 1 to 5
Then expanding the chest
Counting 6 to 10
Hold the breath
Counting 1 to 5
Exhale by relaxing the chest
Counting 1 to 5
Finally relaxing the abdomen
Counting 6 to 10
Repeat 5 to 10 rounds

inhalation and exhalation in step wise manner

variation 1

Try to use the whole passage of the breath
Inhale while mentally counting 1 to 10
Exhale 1 to 3 pausing 4 to 6,

Exhale 7 to 9 pausing 10 to 12
Exhale rest of breath 13 to 15
Repeat 5 to 10 rounds

variation 2

Inhale 1 to 3 pausing 4 to 6
Inhale 7 to 9 pausing 10 to 12
Inhale 13 to 15
Exhale 1 to 3 pausing 4 to 6
Exhale 7 to 9 pausing 10 to 12
Exhale rest of breath 13 to 15
Repeat 5 to 10 rounds

variation 3

Inhale 1 to 3 pausing 4 to 6
Inhale 7 to 9 pausing 10 to 12
Inhale 13 to 15 pausing 16 to 18
Exhale 1 to 3 pausing 4 to 6
Exhale 7 to 9 pausing 10 to 12
Exhale rest of breath 13 to 15 pausing 16 to 18
Repeat 5 to 10 rounds

Try to maintain a smooth flow of breath throughout

PRANAYAMA

It is pranayama which allows prana to flow in harmony, generating heat making the being balanced, light and subtle.

The prana that is flowing at any particular time may be felt by observing the flow of breath in the nostrils.

When the flow is greater in the right nostril, the body generates more heat, after energy is created for physical work, digestion of food and other body processes. If the left nostril flows predominantly while taking food, the digestive process may be slow, causing indigestion.
It is necessary for pranayama that the breath should flow properly through both nostrils. If the right nostril is blocked, then place the right hand in the left armpit and press for a few minutes. Then slowly the right nostril will open. Alternatively one may lie on the left side of the body and the right nostril will slowly open. Repeat on the other side to open the left nostril.

There are a variety of methods for pranayama which we have mentioned but the focus is on **nadishodhan pranyama,** the others being helpful.

Some of these forms consist of a hand position called nasagra mudra.

nasagra mudra

Keep the right hand in front of the face
Place the index and middle fingers gently between the eyebrows
Place the thumb above the right nostril and the ring finger above the left
This will control the flow of breath in the nostrils by pressing on them

kapalbhati pranayama

Sit in a comfortable asana
Become aware of the body
Then bring the awareness to the breath
Adopt the nasagra mudra
Now close the right nostril
Inhale deeply through the left nostril expanding the abdomen
Exhale with 10 forceful contractions of the abdominal muscles
Exhalation can be increased by up to 50 contractions
Do not create any strain
Inhalation should be spontaneous
Then close the left nostril and repeat with the right nostril
Then repeat with both nostrils
Take rest while observing the breath
Repeat 2 to 3 rounds

bhastrika pranayama

Sit in a comfortable asana
Close the eyes and relax the whole body
Adopt the nasagra mudra
Become aware of the breath
Close the right nostril
Now forcefully inhale and exhale through the left nostril 10 times
Expanding and contracting the chest
This can be increased to up to 50 times
Avoid jerking the body
There should be a snuffing sound in the nose
Then close the left nostril and repeat with the right nostril
Then with both nostrils
Take rest while observing the breath
Repeat 2 to 3 rounds

sheetali pranayama

Sit in a comfortable asana
Close the eyes
Relax the whole body
Stick the tongue
Roll it from both sides
Making a tube through the tongue
Inhale deeply while allowing the breath to pass through the tongue

Be aware of the cooling sensation of the breath
Relax the tongue and bring into the mouth
Close the lips
Exhale normally through the nostrils
Repeat 5 to 10 rounds

Some people may not be able to carry out the sheetali pranayama, so seetkali pranayama has been given as an alternative.

seetkari pranayama

Sit in a comfortable asana
Close the eyes
Relax the whole body
Lightly clench the teeth together
Open the lips so the teeth are visible
Inhale deeply while allowing the breath to pass through the teeth
Be aware of the cooling sensation of the breath
Relax the teeth
Close the lips
Exhale normally through the nostrils
Repeat 5 to 10 rounds

brahmari pranayama

Sit in a comfortable asana
Close the eyes
Relax the whole body
Close the ears with the index fingers pressing on the flap
Keep the lips closed
Don't clench the teeth
Inhale deeply through the nostrils
Make a humming sound
Exhalation will occur spontaneously
The humming sound should be smooth and continuous
This will vibrate in the head
Be aware of the vibration
After completing the humming sound
Inhale to repeat next round
Gradually try to increase the length of the humming sound
Repeat 5 to 10 rounds.

ujjayi pranayama

Sit in a comfortable asana
Close the eyes
Relax the whole body
Become aware of the breath
Inhale and exhale deeply through the nostrils

Now bring the awareness to the throat
Feel the breath passing through the throat
Not through the nostrils
Contract the throat muscles
Inhale and allow the breath through the throat
It will create a sound like water passing through a tube
Be aware of the breath passing through the throat
Relax the throat muscles
Exhale normally through the nostrils
Repeat 5 to 10 rounds

walking pranayama

This can be performed during walking. It is better practiced where it is quiet and the air is fresh such as in a park around trees.

Walk with small footsteps
Be aware of the breath and steps
Inhale with 5 steps
Exhale with 5 steps
After a few rounds, the breath will adjust according to the walk.

This can be increased according to one's capacity.

nadishodhan pranayama

The breath should be silent in all techniques of nadishodhana ensuring it is not forced or restricted in any way.
The flow of breath must be smooth with no jerks, throughout the practice.
Remain aware on the breath and counting throughout.

There are many variations with which the nadishodhana pranayama can be carried out. One can perform a variation continuously for 6 to 8 weeks before trying another.

A counting system has been introduced here to help with the length of time for breathing. One can increase the number of counts as the breath capacity increases. Use 'om' with each count to give a more accurate estimate of one second.

The ratio establishes a calming rhythm for the being

Sit in a comfortable asana
Keep the head and spine upright
Close the eyes.
Relax the whole body.
Observe the breath.
Adopt nasagra mudra

breathing with individual nostrils

Close the right nostril
Inhale through the left nostril.
Mentally counting 1 om to 5 om
Exhale through the same nostril
Counting 1 om to 5 om
Close the left nostril and repeat with the right nostril.
Repeat 10 to 15 rounds

breathing in 1:1 (Ratio of inhalation to exhalation)

Close the right nostril
Inhale through the left nostril.
Counting 1 om to 5 om
Then close the left nostril
Exhale through the right nostril
Counting 1 om to 5 om
The time for inhalation and exhalation should be equal.
Repeat inhaling through the right nostril and exhaling through the left nostril.
This is one round
Repeat 10 to 15 rounds

breathing in 1:2

Close the right nostril
Inhale through the left nostril
Counting 1 om to 5 om
Then close the left nostril
Exhale through the right nostril
Counting 1 om to 10 om.
The time for exhalation will be double that of inhalation
Repeat inhaling through the right nostril and exhaling through the left nostril.
Repeat 10 to 15 rounds

breathing in 1:1:1

In this technique internal breath retention is introduced.

Close the right nostril
Inhale through the left nostril
Counting 1 om to 5 om
Hold the breath closing both nostrils
Counting 1 om to 5 om
Close the left nostril
Exhale through the right nostril
Counting 1 om to 5 om
Repeat inhaling through the right nostril
Holding the breath

Exhaling through the left nostril
Repeat 10 to 15 rounds

Other variations of this are summarized in the table below.

Breathing Ratio	Inhale	Internal Retention	Exhale
1:1:2	5 om	5 om	10 om
1:2:2	5 om	10 om	10 om
1:3:2	5 om	15 om	10 om
1:4:2	5 om	20 om	10 om

breathing in 1:1:1:1

In this technique there is both internal and external breath retention

Close the right nostril
Inhale through the left nostril
Counting 1 om to 5om
Holding the breath closing both nostrils
Counting 1 om to 5om
Close the left nostril
Exhale through the right nostril
Counting 1 om to 5 om
Remain closing both nostril
Counting 1 om to 5 om
Repeat inhaling through the right nostril

Holding the breath
Exhaling through the left nostril
Remaining as above
Repeat 10 to 15 rounds

Other variations of this are summarized in the table below.

Breathing Ratio	Inhale	Internal Retention	Exhale	External Retention
1:2:2:1	5 om	10 om	10 om	5 om
1:4:2:1	5 om	20 om	10 om	5 om
1:4:2:2	5 om	20 om	10 om	10 om
1:6:4:2	5 om	30 om	20 om	10 om
1:8:6:4	5 om	40 om	30 om	20 om

Inhaling through the right nostril and exhaling through the left nostril continuously is called **suryabheda pranayama**. This creates heat and makes the being active.

Inhaling through the left nostril and exhaling through the right nostril continuously is called **chandrabheda pranayama**. This calms and allows the being to relax.

THE FLOW OF PRANA

Prana exists not only in the body but in the whole being. It is not necessary that prana is directed only by asana and pranayama, but can be directed through awareness.

Lie on your back in savasana.
Gently close the eyes
Allow the body to be comfortable.
If there is any stiffness then adjust the posture

Be aware of the body
Feel the body on the floor
Feel the clothes the body is wearing
Observe the muscles and joints
Be aware of the heart beat
The blood pulsating
Bring the awareness to the toes and feel the prana flow there
Follow to the heels, ankles calf muscles, knees,
thighs, hips, pelvic region,
abdomen, lower back, spine,
shoulder blades, chest, shoulders, upper arms,
elbows, forearms, wrists, palms and fingers.
Come to the neck, chin, lips, jaw muscles, cheeks,
ears, nose, eyes, forehead, top of the head
and the whole body.

Feel the prana flow throughout the whole body.

Visualise the whole body
Separate from the body
See the body lying on the floor
Become aware of the outside environment
Visualise the floor on which the body is lying
The four walls of the room
The ceiling of the room
The furniture of the room including the body
Slowly come out of the room
Visualise the outside environment
The buildings
The trees
The sky
Become aware of the different sounds
Bring the awareness to the sounds from a far
Move from one sound to another
Motors, bird songs, tree leaves, wind
From gross to subtle
Expanding the awareness

The prana that is working in the cosmos is the same energy that is working in the being.

Now slowly come back to the body
Bring back the awareness to the top of the head
Then slowly throughout the body

The prana is flowing throughout the body.
It is spreading from the top of the head to the face,
neck, shoulders, chest, arms,
back, pelvic region and legs.

Be aware of the whole body
Take 2 to 3 deep breaths
Become aware of the nearby surroundings
Gently move the fingers, hands, legs, neck
Turn to one side
Sit up
Gently open the eyes

HARMONY

Prana is difficult to explain. However, this book aspires to give an understanding of a connection between the body, breath and awareness.

This connection brings the being into a state of harmony.

The practices mentioned can be helpful in this process, but a practice always has limitations. The practices are not equally helpful to everyone as every being's nature is different.

However, as awareness increases these practices will no longer be considered separate from the being but a part of the life processes such as breathing, work, eating, sleep and evolving towards harmony.

Author

Debiprasad, born in 1980, in West Bengal.
He has an MA in Yoga, and since 2002 practices and teaches in
Sri Aurobindo Ashram.